Pulp

poems by

Robert L. Dean, Jr.

Finishing Line Press
Georgetown, Kentucky

Pulp

Copyright © 2022 by Robert L. Dean, Jr.
ISBN 978-1-64662-890-2 First Edition
All rights reserved under International and Pan-American Copyright Conventions. No part of this book may be reproduced in any manner whatsoever without written permission from the publisher, except in the case of brief quotations embodied in critical articles and reviews.

ACKNOWLEDGMENTS

The author gratefully acknowledges the editors and staff of the following publications, in which versions of some of these poems appeared, sometimes in different forms or under different titles:

I-70 Review: "True Romance"
MacQueen's Quinterly: "Doppelgänger," "I Dream I am Chuang Tzu
    Dreaming He is Me Dreaming We are Dalí's Moustache," "Visitor"
October Hill Magazine: "The Caress," "The Tear"
River City Poetry: "Last Supper," "Night Falls," "Pulp," "True Tales of the
    Supernatural," "Worn Out Place"
Shot Glass: "One Fine Fall Day Mr. Pickles Makes a Cameo," "The Scar,"
    "True Confessions"

Publisher: Leah Huete de Maines
Editor: Christen Kincaid
Cover Art: Martha Wherry
Author Photo: Cole Dean
Cover Design: Elizabeth Maines McCleavy

Order online: www.finishinglinepress.com
        also available on amazon.com

Author inquiries and mail orders:
Finishing Line Press
PO Box 1626
Georgetown, Kentucky 40324
USA

Table of Contents

Pulp 1

True Romance 2

The Tear 3

Night Falls... 4

True Crime 6

Motherless Child 7

Worn Out Place 8

Doppelgänger 11

True Tales of the Supernatural 13

The Scar 15

Visitor... 16

True Confessions 18

Guitar 19

Last Supper 20

The Caress.. 21

I Dream I am Chuang Tzu Dreaming He is Me Dreaming
    We Are Dalí's Moustache.. 22

True Detective 23

The Sigh 25

Icarus' Mother 26

A Brief History of Human Flight... 27

Bela Lugosi in the Off-hours 29

One Fine Fall Day Mr. Pickles Makes a Cameo 30

For Dolores Granger

"There's no place it doesn't exist."

Chuang Tzu's answer to Master Tung-kuo when asked by the latter, where does "this thing called the Way" exist? Section twenty-two of the Chuang Tzu, translated by Burton Watson.

Pulp

You could
draw and quarter it,
chuck it in the blender,
but what you really want,
with this autumn night
peering wide-eyed in your boudoir window,
is your fingernails clawing
the rind, the pebbly skin peeling back
into the cup of your palm, and only then
do you section it, careful like a surgeon entering
a body, suck the tit of each segment, the blood
of the mandarin trickling down your chin like
orgasm, the pulp sweet on your tongue, heaven dripping

onto the open book in your lap, Li Po's *Jade Stairs Lament*
tearing up right where *Night, late, has its way with her
silken hose,* but you resist dropping your many-faceted curtain,
reach instead for another fruit, another life, another moon,
tome of the fruit of life, the most ancient *Shijing,* and when you bite
    into
the first ode—the one where the prince seeks but doesn't find
the modest, retiring, virtuous, young lady—a November breeze
whispers down from Cold Mountain
of temple bells rung, drums beat, stone chimes struck, and you reach
    back
yet another life, you are Cai Lun discovering the distillation
of paper out of mulberry bark, the stuff upon which
the fall of your very first crystal curtain will be written, how, after you
cause the deaths of Consort Song and her sister by their own hands,
you bathe, don your finest silk robe, and swallow
the poison of your own making rather than surrender
to the Emperor's blind-eyed, dark moon prison, the stuff, surely,

of a Spicy Detective, Startling Stories, Weird Tales, Black Mask.
You suckle another slice and turn the page.

True Romance

It's the Blue Room
on a weeping ebony
night and jazz cries
out from the bell of the

sax, moans from the
friction points where
the bassist's fingers
attack the strings, whispers

up from the caress of
wire whisks across
the skin of the snare,
bleeds in soft wounds

of magenta and lapis
from yarned heads
of mallets kissing
cold metal bars,

permeates the pin-
drop air with But
Beautiful, and I'm thinking
the lyrics got it wrong,

it's not funny *or* sad,
tearful *or* gay, it's
and, but if you fall
you fall, oh yeah,

they got that part right
as I drain the dregs
of a Jack & Coke, stare past
the band, 18th & Vine

dripping with the absence of you.

The Tear

Not yet an ocean, a stream, just a drop, slipping over
the lip of your lid, a glistening hesitation on the

black silk threads of your lash, a tiny globe in which
I see myself, glancing back upstream toward the iris

green source, the black wellspring of the depths of
you, of us, the storm front of whatever I have said or done

occluding the pearly sky of your soul, the hail yet to
pummel, the twister yet to descend, just this one lone jewel,

falling, finally, rivering my heart down the Rushmore of
your cheek, a pitch my fingertips remember from drier

days, pausing at the mouth hinge where I so often
seek refuge, where you have drunk me in so many times,

but now I race on, unlevied, plunge, at last, and, it seems,
forever, from the threshold of your face, wondering,

is this how it ends, what drowning feels like, or do we simply
run this rapid, flood these narrows, conquer this cataract,

find our own level in the delta of apology, lose the silt of ourselves
in some sea of reconciliation, sip fresh breezes of what we were,

where we started, the soft expectant calm before the storm,
the sun birthing bloody and naked in the horizons of our eyes.

Night Falls

doors slam behind you
behind me doors retaliate

closing
slamming
do doors ever

open
whisper
the stars now ghosts
in our eyes
do we ever

find the key to what is us
stop this endless leaving
exit Exit X IT out
so many

doors
wide open when we moved in
one by one
we chop them down
kindle the pyre of misunderstanding
understanding all too well

the squeaky hinge
jamb out of plumb
cracked lintel
mislaid tools
the hiding of them sometimes

can we
feel the knob in our hands
comprehend the certainty of it

can we
turn it as if life depends on the turning
as if lives

in our eyes
night falls
and we turn

which way now

True Crime

The naked heart is a loaded gun. Words chamber there
like shells, like bullets, waiting for the ventricular shotgun pump,
the vagus nerve hammer-cock that will load them into
the barrel of the throat, explode them from the muzzle of

the mouth, lodge them like smoldering sniper sights
at the backs of the eyes, ready to tracer out, take down
you, passing stranger who does not pass, who ignores the
Keep Out language of this, the country of my body. Death

litters my days, the wounded bleed out in nightmare
stretchers. Somebody calls for a medic, an ambulance.
I look away from the killing field. Blood beats the drums
of my ears. I did not mean it, I blubber under such
third degree. Accident. Hair trigger. The detective

isn't convinced, knows all my dirty little secrets,
points to a rap sheet the length of eternity.
The detective is a loaded gun, beating, beating,
beating. The fingerprints on the rubber hose

he wields match the crime scene. Our atria
bear the same serial number. The tell-tale heart
tells all. He is the murderer. I am the murderer. We are
the murderer. Our name is Cain. We get off one last shot:

Mercy

But the dead are bulletproof, and we are bound, led
to the scaffold where the hangman waits, his life blood
beating BrotherBrotherBrother between our shoulder blades
as he slips on noose, hood. Spent projectiles, we fall.

The earth does not receive us.

Motherless Child

Inside a robin's egg
this must be what it looks like
to look up

fragile vault
virginal
as spring water

flowing through
an other's eye

crisp fall day
sugar maple sparks
in the ring around
the open aperture
which drinks me in
or am I falling

from some neglected nest
which I should have flown
when pear buds burst white

and if this sky shell shatters
will the wind coo
there now

whose wings will swoop
to this hatchling wreck
poke fat grubs

down my
begging beak

let it be you
my other eye

Worn Out Place

that rut
in the carpet
of my soul

worry
worry
worry

and back again

can't you see it
careful don't fall in
quarantine old hat

for me
I shall not want
a shepherd

the world out of kilter
behind me
slams shut
a table
prepares itself
in the absence of mine enemies

anointing
I shall not want

the sheep
rattle chains
if only
you could hear them

a ghost I am
raggedy
threadbare
fluttering in the attic
of sanity

all the empty-hearted
drafty places
familiar
it's my attic
after all
the world never visits

spring
summer
fall
winter

never knock
never wave back

I shall not want

don't attempt
to tempt me

off my ledge
out of my furrow

yea I walk the valley
shadow death
fear thou art with me
rod and staff

yea though I thread
again
the worn-out place

I shall not want
green pastures
waters still
mine enemies cup
overrun
mercy all the days
in this house
I dwell

I shall
not want
righteousness

restoreth my soul
never
merciless all the nights

worry
worry
worry

can't you see it
O can't you

Doppelgänger

Shadow walks ahead
I'm always chasing
rainbows double arced

as if it had rained here
as if the clocks had never
stopped saluting time

passing through yesterday
only a rumor tomorrow
the train that never arrives

whistling a Rock Island tune
in the dripping dark my brother
rolls beside me into sleep

from the north room
Grandma snores in German
pancakes and Log Cabin syrup

is what the sun smells like rising
afternoon the sugar cookies bloom
into the tick-tock mantelpiece warning

whispers of impending chalkboard doom
Miss Buttenhof babbling away
signs and cosigns fractioning

like burst cloud streamers
blues greens magentas
this day that day the next

it never rains here anymore
shadow floats ahead a mirage
I thirst from this cross

of streets unfamiliar now
as always all too soon
I'll catch up taste what only

shadow knows the world
beneath my feet but this one
violet-scented day the sky

double arced like eyes
in wrinkled skin
leaks memory

and shadow
sizzling
dances on

True Tales of the Supernatural

You don't pass through the cold
spot, it passes through you. You look
at the gauges: nothing. Check the
video monitor: more nothing. Something

abnormally paranormal about
this investigation. You reconnoiter
your surroundings. You don't
recognize this house, you've never

been here before, yet there's that
old baby crib you've seen pictures of
with you wrapped in diapers, the
ladder of pencil marks on the door

jamb where your dad recorded
your passage to manhood, much to
you mother's chagrin, and that—
no, it can't be. Margie Cranston's

bra! Only that was at the drive-in,
one of those Son of Flubber or
Nutty Professor movies, or at least
that's what you told them when the folks

granted you the keys on that first full moon
after the last ladder mark, though what you
really saw was a quick flash of Mrs. Robinson's
tits, and you timed your maneuver accordingly

since you'd seen the flick three times already
at the Orpheum—there's a parking lot
there now—and what's that God-awful moaning
coming from down the hall or whatever it is

you're standing in, some doorway to hell
maybe, you float down to see, look in
the open door and it's You and the first
Mrs. You, wrestling away in that crummy

bed in your first cheap apartment and yes,
that was some kind of hell alright, but
Orpheus-like you escaped and of course
you wouldn't have Becky if it wasn't for

that night of fingernails dug in, ash tray shards
on the hardwood, that night of backs to each
other afterwards, those years of nights and days
of hot words, cold shoulders, a shudder runs down

your spine, cobwebs kiss your face, you reach out
towards that light way down there, white, warm,
pulsing, like the strobe at the disco where you met
the second Mrs. You, reach out, grasping: nothing.

You remember now. Last week, the booze, the fight.
Yesterday— You check the gauges: nothing. The monitor:
nothing. At the end of the hall, a bathroom, a mirror—
you remember because it was the last thing you

saw in that dingy motel after the breakup, the razor
slicing across your throat. Now you have your bearings.
You know where you are. You are home. That nothing,
it's all that's left of the ladder of you. And you hope, as you

enter the light, that
Becky understands.

The Scar

I feel them on the inside
of your mouth, run my tongue
over the tattooed history of you.

Nightmares, you say. I want to
cast them out but you refuse
to believe I am your Christ

and there are no swine passing
by and, indeed, I have no gash
in my side for your doubts to probe.

I turn my head to tell you tonight
you'll be with me in paradise. You
suck in your cheeks and bite down,

eyes wide. I rebuke the storm and still
you quake. Water into wine, nothing.
My last miracle. Your next scar.

Visitor

When you walk through
the door of me
which way
are the geese
flying

what hour
do the clocks chime
are they in unison
I always forget
to wind them

straighten the pictures
if the walls stare at you
out of plumb

sandwiches
are waiting
in the kitchen
forgive me

if they are stale
I've always known you were coming
just not the day
the epoch
or who

you will say that you are
what name you will call out

when you see me
lurking
all of my

cobwebs
secret panels
groaning pipes
cold spots
scent of lavender

and something
you can't quite
put your finger on

such a crying shame as
I've always counted on
your finger
to point me to

who built this house
how long it has been here
how long

before the roof falls in
and where I hid
the key

True Confessions

In broad daylight
I murder you with words. But
my body, oh, my body
lives you nightly. Your eyes
like starlight whisper

through the undraped windows
of my soul, lick a sinuous Milky
Way of sweat-spangled skin.
Your mouth a supernova. You
a universe, unreason expanding

and you open yourself, become infinite
space, let the everything of me
slip in. The cold metal voice of regret rises
yet another morning.

Guitar

You stroke silver strings
stars sing beneath
slender fingers

fill the sky
of my nights
and for as long as the song

lasts
I am music

now from your mouth the moon
just as I reach out to
grasp it the sky falls

silent
total eclipse
ice clinks

in my glass
in the dark
such a

brief affair

Last Supper

You need not have stolen
this heart was yours
always
for the asking
wind sun moon rain
would you thieve these also
even the fox dare not
the stars are safe
from the unkindness of ravens

one tear shed
in spring
lady-in-a-bath
valentine wine
dripping
unbidden
from the hem of her
crimson petaled kimono
cupped hands
all you need
to taste
the salt of it
she does not look to see
who
accepts the offering
ask
what need you have of it
what care
you will take of it

would you think
me not so generous as
the lilies of the field

O ye of little faith

take, eat
do this in remembrance of me

The Caress

Day creeps about the room
my hand reaches out
crosses
continents
solar systems
galaxies
time
all of time
a forever of stopped clocks
page-less calendars
suns standing still
ten thousand trumpets blast
walls fall
Jericho is empty
in the night you have slipped away
morning sleeps on your pillow
where were the watchmen
the sentries
my fist closes around
the vacancy of you
your skin
a memory on my fingertips
the cleft of my lifeline
teases me
the heart line impossible to read
I caress
the nothing lying next to me
naked
cold
eternal
this was love
yes
this was
or so we said

I Dream I am Chuang Tzu Dreaming He Is Me Dreaming We Are Dalí's Moustache

watches melt
fluid faces
time / memory slinks
across the furniture
I rise up creaking
old / young
I was
when The Dreaming
laid me down
perchance to sleep / to flutter
butterfly
nightmares
in the
window-
painted sun
whisper / rattle
deep in my throat
dawn dies
how brief the light
this house
this coffin
/ soul
each rusty day a nail / lepidoptera pin
creation dripping
dripping
drip-
ping

True Detective

I'm on the trail of
the Queen of Hearts.
I don't know her name
or what she looks like.
I've been told she lives
only in shadows and abandoned
houses and in certain scenes
on the big screen
like when Bogart tells Bacall
Go ahead, scratch.

I turn up the collar of
my trench coat against the
numb night of there, then.
I've turned all the heres, nows,
upside down and inside
out and I'm going, going,
gone cause every time
the phone rings there's no one

there, except I think maybe I hear
breathing, and then I realize it's
me, just me, with an itch,
and I think back to
how I got on this job, remember
I've always been on this job, I'll always
be on this job, it's my breathing

on both ends, I'm not just the
dick, I'm the mark, chattering away
to myself in some obscure silent
flicker to which all the inter titles
have been lost and the director
was strangled in the middle of yelling
cut and that's me, too. And the dame,

well, she's the Black Bird
that Bogey holds up at the end
of the picture and quotes
Shakespeare over, that drivel about
dreams. Only a sucker buys hooey
like that. I run my fingers
over the Fat Man's pocket knife scars,
sense I'm close to something, only to feel
it slip away. You got it. Me again. Only I
go on forever, scratching. A cold, cold case.

The Sigh

Winter heaves up from the bone yard,
shivers the fruit of a tamarind tree,
weeps across the eye of the moon, rains down
upon Mount Kikizi, swims northward to spawn
the pyramids, whispers across the sea

to drowning Venice. A gondolier
in bleeding sash steers a tourist, serenades
a span of shuddering suspiration. The pilgrim plunders
the bridge with Nikon lens, wings west
across Atlantis, sows seeds of sorrow
amongst the sunflowers.

Eons pass. The sigh returns to dust. Then today

stale breaths exhale from leaves
of a cracked-spine photo album you excavate
from the catacombs of a closet, along with
a ragged crow's feather and faded letters
from Little Rock. It's spring housecleaning and
you want to know about these things, the world
before you.

Ice caps melt. In Amazonas butterfly wings
flap.

You-less, there is no world.
Was never. I breathe
back in the sigh. Bury it
deeper in the marrow.

Icarus' Mother

From this aery portico
anyone else would pray for sail
billowing into harbor
but she's upturned to sky
or where sky was
before Phoebus boiled her eyes
watch the sky the papyrus said
she doesn't recall the
harbinger signet why
no one asks her name
that too gone
the thermodynamics of wax escape her
the fickleness of feathers at altitude
the hubris of youth
the treachery of men
a flicker just
behind her the temple
around her the Acropolis
falls and rises and falls
pigeons coo and flutter
brood after brood of
jackboots
shell casings
each time they rebuild
the goddess thunks more hollow
they model it after old what's-'er-name
every millennium or so
a drachma clinks at her feet every
war revolution day
parched sockets trickle
the splatter of another mother's child
someone should tell her
christen her a constellation
Apteros Nike
lighten this dark place
where flight deconstructs

A Brief History of Human Flight

The flaw in that Icarus story
is not proximity to the sun,
but the weight of radius and ulna.

Strap on all the feathers you want
and you're still not getting off the ground,
not unless you bore some bone out, graft in

a few air pockets. Spruce and muslin
and a scintilla of internal combustion
carried Orville and Wilbur ten feet

closer to the gods for a wobbly
twelve seconds. Four sandwiches,
two canteens and a pot to piss in

christened the luck in Lucky Lindy. Amelia
whistled, gap-toothed, into her radio,
said *We will repeat this message…wait,*

then zagged into the Twilight Zone.
Grace is simply not a part
of the human flight curriculum. Hence

vomit bags and meclizine, vacuum toilets,
oxygen masks blitzing
from the overhead, B17s fire storming

Wagner's Dresden and Brahms' Hamburg
with recycled master discs of Mississippi
John Hurt and Louis Armstrong. At least

we gold plated Blind Willie Johnson
and Voyagered him into space.
But what will the Arcturans think

when they hear that ghost track
we picked for posterity,
"Dark was the Night, Cold was the Ground"?

Will they want to hang
with us on the veranda,
suck down a Bud Lite, gaze up

at that veiled fickle mistress, moon,
and listen to our musings on
how it was with Neal and Buzz and

One Small Step for Man? And what *do* we tell them
about Icarus? That he flapped and flapped
like a lead-footed ostrich

until his father—a big, raw-boned working stiff
from what we hear tell—said *the hell with it*
and hopped a tramp trireme for sunnier climes?

Or do we dial up Blind Willie
on some rogue radio wave,
stretch ourselves out

on the star bereft airdrome of arctic audacity,
hand a Black & Decker
to one of the little green men, and,

in our best Henny Youngman voice,
say
Take my marrow, please...

Bela Lugosi in the Off-hours

night opens a window
dreams flutter in
shed moon wove robes
unravel threads

of logic
knit new memories
in which I clothe
the past

the future
sinks vampire teeth
into the present
writhing I

hold on
for dear life

One Fine Fall Day Mr. Pickles Makes a Cameo

John's Animal World
has closed its doors. Ridden,
gut shot, into the sunset. Ahead

looms winter like the Teton massif.
Road kill litters the highway.
Geese explode lake calm,

skim the mirror's surface.
Seared against the beetling sky
reflections swarm like gnats.

Caught in the spokes
of memory, a hamster
lies, twitching.

Come back, John.
Come back.

Robert L. Dean, Jr. is the author of *The Aerialist Will not be Performing: ekphrastic poems and short fictions to the art of Steven Schroeder* (Turning Plow Press, 2020), and *At the Lake with Heisenberg* (Spartan Press, 2018). A multiple *Best of the Net* nominee and a *Pushcart* nominee, his work has appeared in *October Hill Magazine; Flint Hills Review; I-70 Review; Chiron Review; The Ekphrastic Review; Shot Glass; Illya's Honey; Red River Review; KYSO Flash; MacQueen's Quinterly; River City Poetry; Heartland!* and *the Wichita Broadside Project*. Dean is event coordinator for *Epistrophy: An Afternoon of Poetry and Improvised Music*, held annually in Wichita, Kansas. A native Kansan, Dean studied music composition with Dr. Walter Mays at Wichita State University before going on the road as a bass player, conductor, and arranger; he was a professional musician for 30 years, playing with acts such as Jesse Lopez, Bo Didley, Frank Sinatra Jr., Vic Damone, Jim Stafford, Kenny Rankin, B. W. Stevenson, the Dallas Jazz Orchestra, and putting in a stint in the house band at the Fairmont Hotel Venetian Room in Dallas. While living in Dallas, he also put in 20 years working for The Dallas Morning News and made the transition from music to writing before moving back to Kansas in 2007. He lives in a one-hundred-year-old stone building in Augusta, Kansas, along with a universe of books, CDs, LPs, an electric bass, and a couple dozen hats. In his spare time, he practices the time-honored art of hermitry.

www.ingramcontent.com/pod-product-compliance
Lightning Source LLC
LaVergne TN
LVHW041508070426
835507LV00012B/1402